My Mother and Me

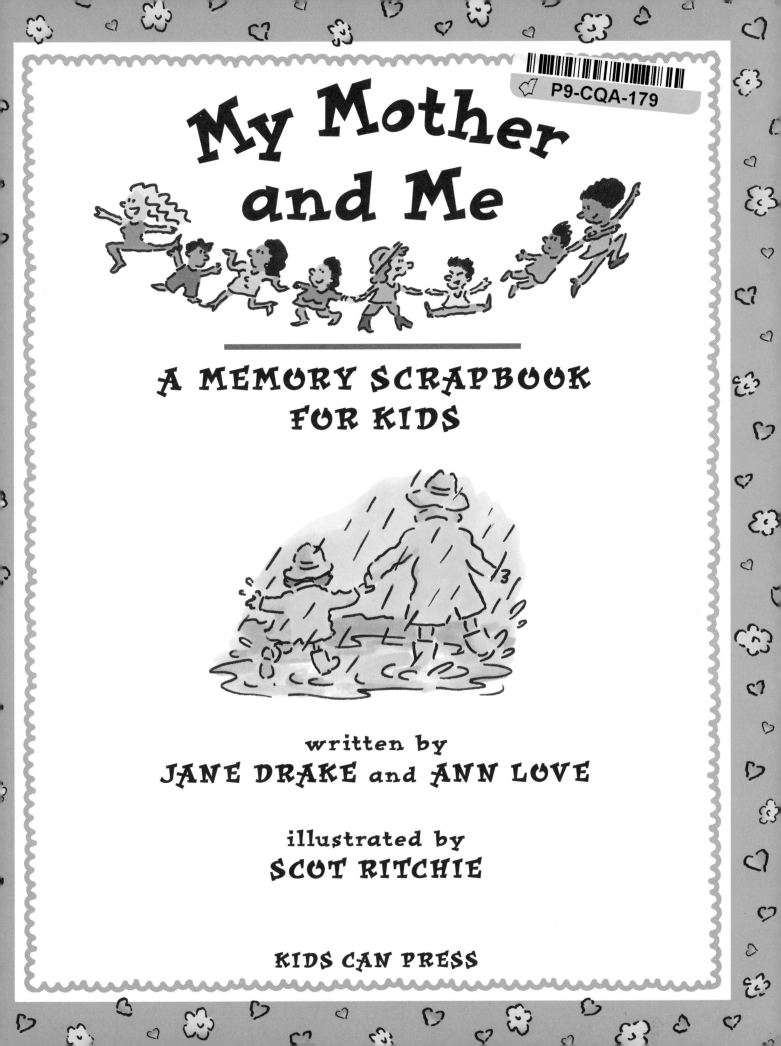

A MEMORY SCRAPBOOK FOR KIDS

written by

JANE DRAKE and **ANN LOVE**

illustrated by

SCOT RITCHIE

KIDS CAN PRESS

My Mother and Me

My name is _____.

My mother's special name for me is _____.

I was born on _____ _____, _____.
                          (month)   *(day)*   *(year)*

I am _____ years old.

I was born in _____, _____.
               (city/town)   *(country)*

I am my mother's

☐ oldest child

☐ youngest child

☐ only child

☐ second child

☐ _____

My mother's name is _____.

My special name for my mother is _____.

My mother was born on _____ _____, _____.
                                  (month)   *(day)*   *(year)*

She is _____ years old.

She was born in _____, _____.
                    (city/town)   *(country)*

In her family, my mother is the

- [ ] oldest child
- [ ] youngest child
- [ ] only child
- [ ] second child
- [ ] _____

When I Was Little

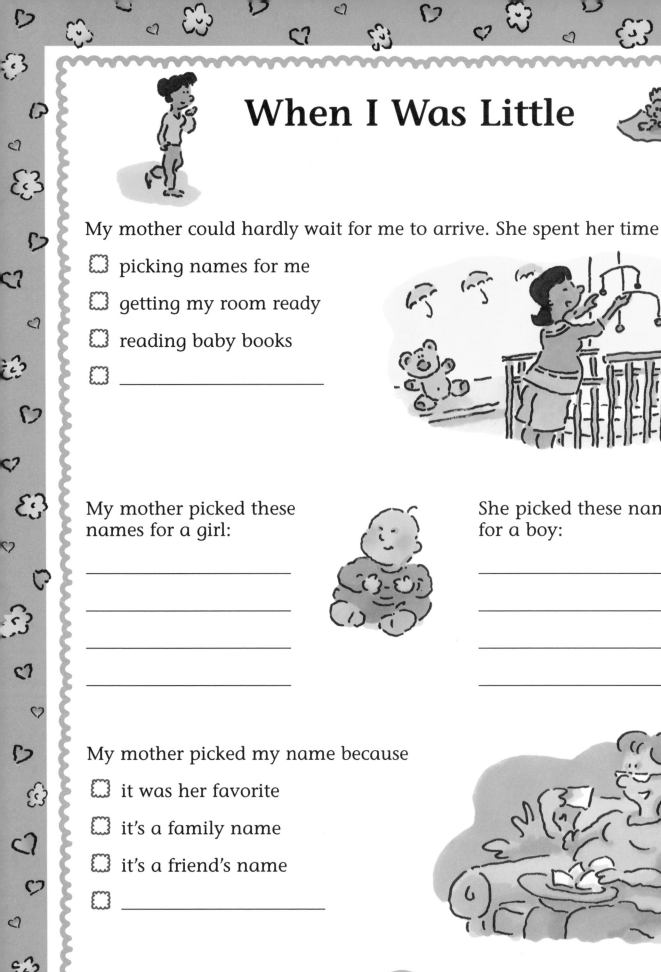

My mother could hardly wait for me to arrive. She spent her time

☐ picking names for me

☐ getting my room ready

☐ reading baby books

☐ _____

My mother picked these names for a girl:

_____

_____

_____

_____

She picked these names for a boy:

_____

_____

_____

_____

My mother picked my name because

☐ it was her favorite

☐ it's a family name

☐ it's a friend's name

☐ _____

When I arrived home, the first thing my mother and I did was

☐ sleep   ☐ cuddle and rock   ☐ _____

☐ eat   ☐ look at each other

When I was little, my mother and I loved to

☐ walk through puddles

☐ snuggle up with a story

☐ swing in the park

☐ _____

Here's a picture of my mother and me when I was little:

Our Family Tree

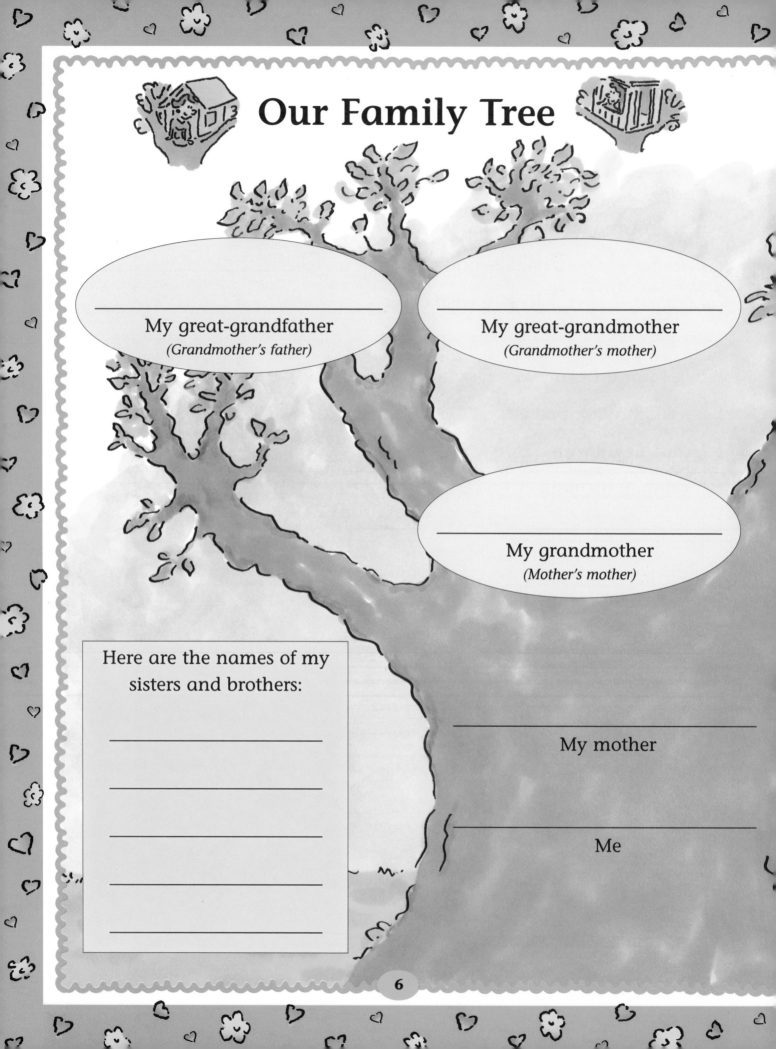

My great-grandfather
(Grandmother's father)

My great-grandmother
(Grandmother's mother)

My grandmother
(Mother's mother)

Here are the names of my sisters and brothers:

_____

_____

_____

_____

_____

My mother

Me

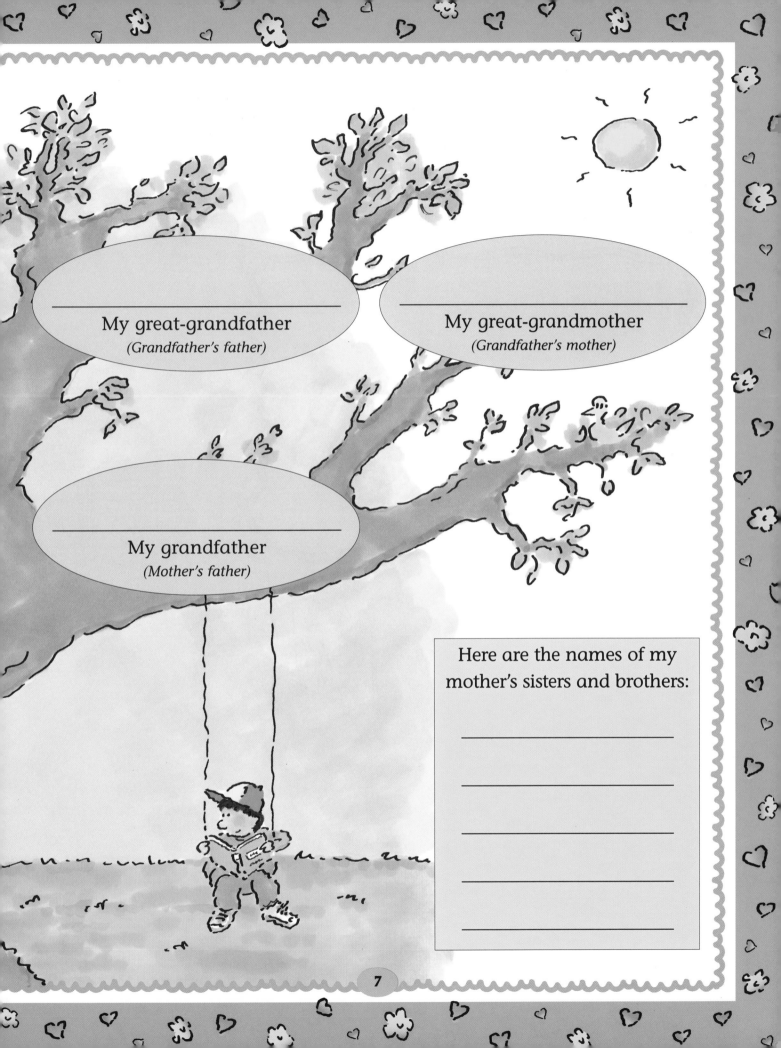

_____
My great-grandfather
(Grandfather's father)

_____
My great-grandmother
(Grandfather's mother)

_____
My grandfather
(Mother's father)

Here are the names of my
mother's sisters and brothers:

_____

_____

_____

_____

_____

Two Peas in a Pod

Here's a picture of my mother and me:

My mother and I look

☐ a little bit alike

☐ a lot alike

☐ nothing alike

We both have

☐ skinny legs

☐ small eyes

☐ big cheeks

☐ _____

I wish I had my mother's

☐ hair

☐ smile

☐ teeth

☐ _____

My mother wishes she had my

☐ nose

☐ eyelashes

☐ knees

☐ _____

Everyone says I look like my mother when I am

☐ sleeping

☐ running

☐ happy

☐ _____

When my mother and I stand side by side, I come up to her _____.

Here is my mother's thumbprint, and here's mine beside it:

At Home

Our home is
- ☐ an apartment
- ☐ a trailer
- ☐ a house
- ☐ _____

- ☐ in the country
- ☐ by the sea
- ☐ in a city
- ☐ _____

Our home is just like us. It's
- ☐ busy
- ☐ messy
- ☐ tidy

- ☐ quiet
- ☐ noisy
- ☐ _____

My mother and I love being at home together.

Here's what we like to do the most *(circle the pictures)*:

I help my mother around the house.

Here are some of the jobs I do *(circle the pictures)*:

The job my mother and I like the most is _____.

The chore we don't like at all is _____.

When our work is done we like to

☐ eat a snack

☐ go for a walk

☐ have a snooze

☐ _____

Out and About Together

My mother and I like to explore places close to home.

Here's a map of our neighborhood:

In our neighborhood, we've got lots of

☐ cats   ☐ kangaroos   ☐ squirrels

☐ kids   ☐ trees   ☐ _____

Our favorite neighbor is _____.

Our favorite place in the neighborhood is _____.

My mother and I like to explore the city. We sometimes see *(circle the pictures)*

When we're out together, we like to

☐ visit the farmer's market   ☐ see a movie

☐ watch trains go by   ☐ go to the sports arena

☐ go swimming   ☐ _____

Here are some souvenirs I've collected on my trips with my mother:

Our Favorite Things

Favorite Things	My List	My Mother's List
Color	_____	_____
Clothes	_____	_____
TV show	_____	_____
Movie	_____	_____
Song	_____	_____
Book	_____	_____
Sport	_____	_____

Favorite Things	My List	My Mother's List
Time of the day	_____	_____
Month	_____	_____
Season	_____	_____
Weather	_____	_____
Animal	_____	_____
Bug	_____	_____
Flower	_____	_____

Meals and Manners

Here is a picture of the best meal my mother makes *(draw on the plate)*:

I help my mother with the meals by

- ☐ setting the table
- ☐ peeling the vegetables
- ☐ stirring the soup

- ☐ tasting the dessert
- ☐ supervising
- ☐ _____

Between meals, my mother and I munch on *(circle the pictures)*

When we're eating, we

- ☐ talk about our day
- ☐ watch TV
- ☐ tell funny stories
- ☐ _____

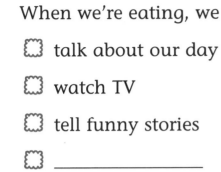

My mother always tells me

- ☐ "Don't talk with your mouth full."
- ☐ "Keep your elbows off the table."
- ☐ "Use your knife and fork."
- ☐ _____

At the table, my mother is happy when I

- ☐ try new foods
- ☐ ask for seconds
- ☐ chew slowly
- ☐ _____

She's not so happy when I

- ☐ burp
- ☐ spill my milk
- ☐ feed the dog from my plate
- ☐ _____

Fun and Games

My mother and I really have fun when we

- ☐ play catch
- ☐ build a fort
- ☐ pretend we're pirates
- ☐ paint pictures
- ☐ _____

Our favorite game is

- ☐ snakes and ladders
- ☐ badminton
- ☐ crazy eights
- ☐ _____

I always win when we play _____.

My mother always wins when we play _____.

My favorite hobby is

- [ ] drawing
- [ ] collecting stones
- [ ] building things
- [ ] _____

My mother's favorite hobby is

- [ ] building birdhouses
- [ ] stargazing
- [ ] line dancing
- [ ] _____

Sometimes my mother and I make things together.

Here's a picture of one of the things we made:

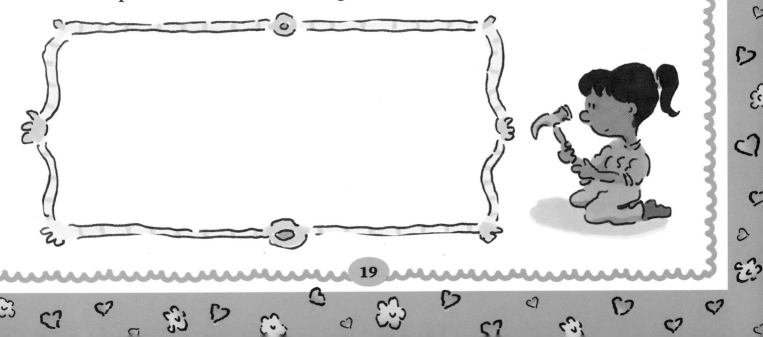

Time for Bed

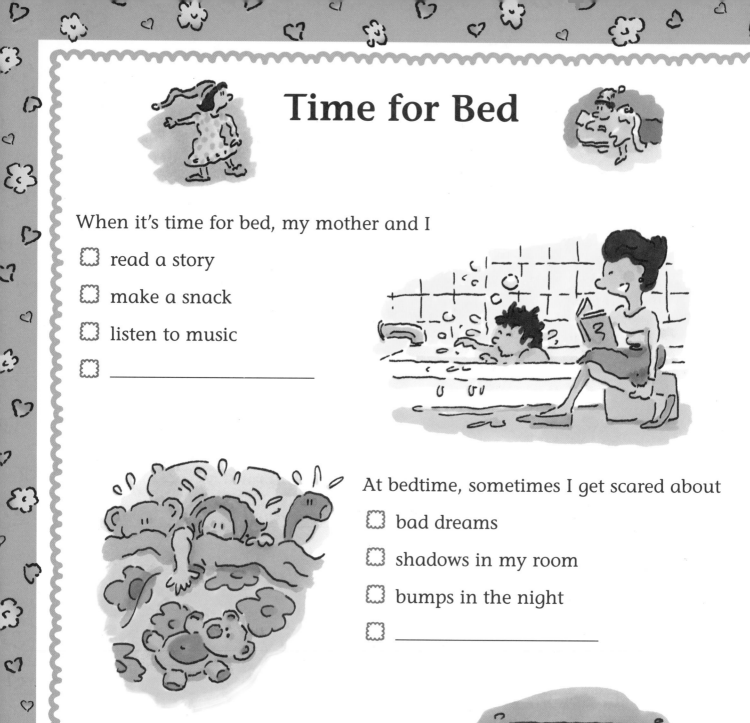

When it's time for bed, my mother and I

☐ read a story

☐ make a snack

☐ listen to music

☐ _____

At bedtime, sometimes I get scared about

☐ bad dreams

☐ shadows in my room

☐ bumps in the night

☐ _____

When I'm scared, my mother

☐ stays with me

☐ looks for monsters

☐ turns on a night light

☐ _____

Each night, the last thing I say to my mother is

☐ "May I have a drink?"

☐ "Please leave the light on."

☐ "One more hug, please."

☐ "I love you."

☐ _____

At bedtime, the last thing my mother says to me is

☐ "Sleep tight!"

☐ "Sweet dreams."

☐ "Lights out!"

☐ "I love you."

☐ _____

In the morning,

☐ my mother wakes me up

☐ I wake my mother up

☐ the alarm clock wakes us up

☐ my dog licks my face

☐ _____

Good Days, Bad Days

My mother and I have lots of good days together. Here's a picture of us on one of the best days we ever had:

This is what I remember most about that day:

_____

_____

This is what my mother remembers most about that day:

_____

_____

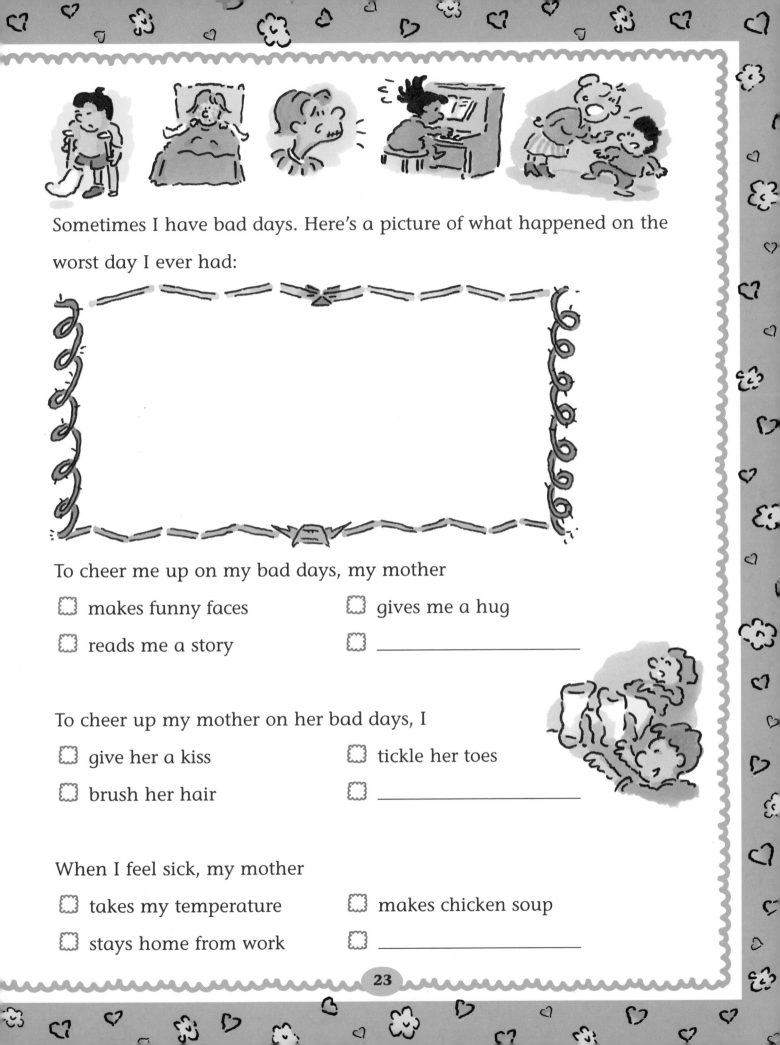

Sometimes I have bad days. Here's a picture of what happened on the worst day I ever had:

To cheer me up on my bad days, my mother

- [ ] makes funny faces
- [ ] reads me a story
- [ ] gives me a hug
- [ ] _____

To cheer up my mother on her bad days, I

- [ ] give her a kiss
- [ ] brush her hair
- [ ] tickle her toes
- [ ] _____

When I feel sick, my mother

- [ ] takes my temperature
- [ ] stays home from work
- [ ] makes chicken soup
- [ ] _____

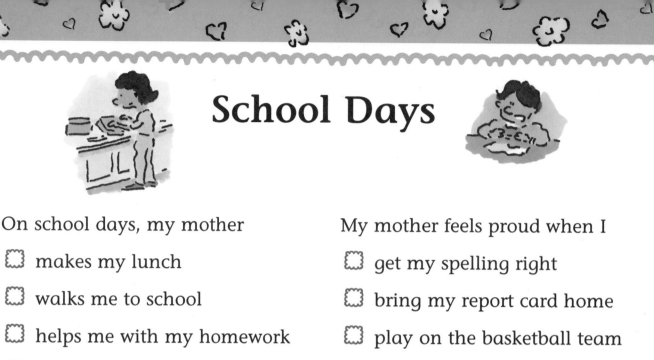

School Days

On school days, my mother

- ☐ makes my lunch
- ☐ walks me to school
- ☐ helps me with my homework
- ☐ asks me what I did all day
- ☐ _____

My mother feels proud when I

- ☐ get my spelling right
- ☐ bring my report card home
- ☐ play on the basketball team
- ☐ sing in the school choir
- ☐ _____

My favorite activity at school is *(circle the pictures)*

My mother comes to my school

☐ to visit my classroom

☐ to watch a concert

☐ for a class trip

☐ _____

My mother says it was different when she went to school because

☐ only girls learned to sew

☐ there were no computers

☐ she played marbles at recess

☐ _____

Here's something I made for my mother at school:

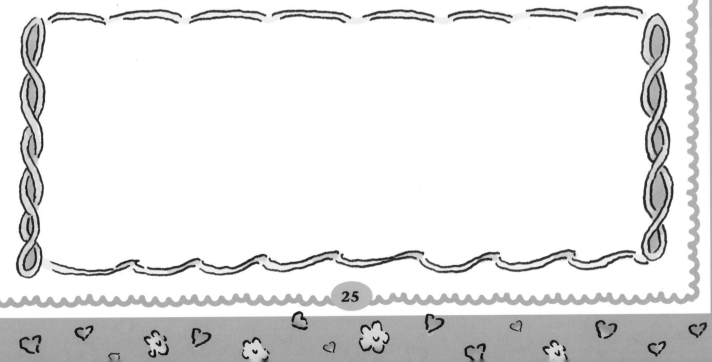

Holidays and Celebrations

My mother and I love to celebrate special days together.

Our favorite time to celebrate is

- [ ] Halloween
- [ ] Christmas
- [ ] Eid
- [ ] Kwanzaa
- [ ] Hanukkah
- [ ] the New Year
- [ ] our birthdays
- [ ] _____

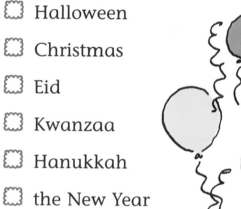

The best part of our celebration is _____.

We eat lots of _____.

We wear _____.

We usually invite _____.

Here are some of the things we've collected from our celebrations:

Show and Tell

My mother always tells me

- ☐ "Clean your room."
- ☐ "Have fun!"
- ☐ "Take out the garbage."
- ☐ "You're a special kid."
- ☐ _____

My mother showed me how to

- ☐ use a screwdriver
- ☐ ride a bike
- ☐ peel a carrot
- ☐ tie my shoes
- ☐ skip rope
- ☐ _____

My mother's favorite saying is

- ☐ "You can do it!"
- ☐ "Awesome!"
- ☐ "You're kidding!"
- ☐ _____

I always tell my mother

☐ "I'm not tired."

☐ "You're the best mom in the world."

☐ "Don't forget your keys."

☐ "I'll be famous when I grow up."

☐ _____

I showed my mother how to

☐ kick a ball

☐ play chess

☐ yodel

☐ hold a hamster

☐ ride a horse

☐ _____

My favorite saying is

☐ "No way!"

☐ "Cool!"

☐ "All right!"

☐ _____

Stories About Us

My mother tells me great stories. Her stories are about

- ☐ when she was a girl
- ☐ when I was a baby
- ☐ wild places
- ☐ exciting adventures
- ☐ _____

My mother tells this story about me:

_____

_____

_____

_____

When my mother tells me a story, I

- ☐ watch her face
- ☐ sit on her knee
- ☐ hug my teddy
- ☐ _____

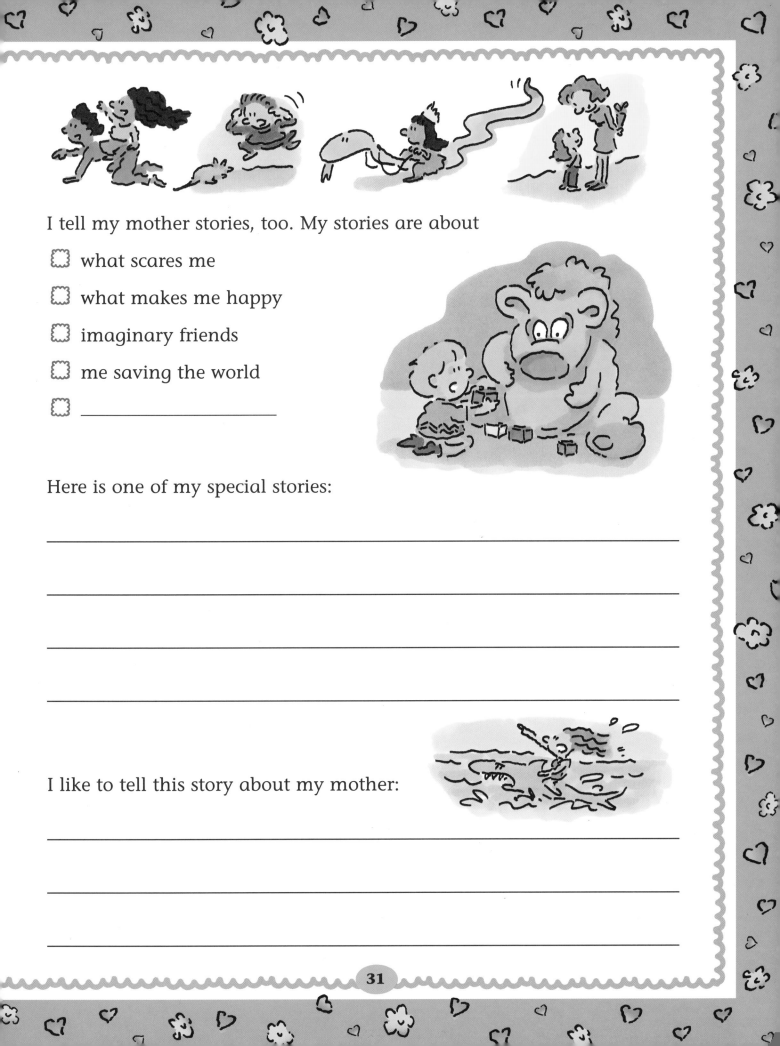

I tell my mother stories, too. My stories are about

☐ what scares me

☐ what makes me happy

☐ imaginary friends

☐ me saving the world

☐ _____

Here is one of my special stories:

_____

_____

_____

_____

I like to tell this story about my mother:

_____

_____

_____

Text © 2000 Jane Drake and Ann Love
Illustrations © 2000 Scot Ritchie

Kids Can Press acknowledges the support of the Government of Canada,
through the BPIDP, for our publishing activity.

Published in Canada by
Kids Can Press Ltd.
29 Birch Avenue
Toronto, ON M4V 1E2

Published in the U.S. by
Kids Can Press Ltd.
2250 Military Road
Tonawanda, NY 14150

www.kidscanpress.com

Designed by Julia Naimska

Printed in Hong Kong, China, by Wing King Tong Company Limited

CM 00   0 9 8 7 6 5

ISBN 1-55074-635-9

Kids Can Press is a *corus*™ Entertainment company